BERNARDO DE
GÁLVEZ
Hero of the American Revolution

BERNARDO DE GÁLVEZ

Hero of the American Revolution

By

Lorenzo G. LaFarelle

EAKIN PRESS ★ Austin, Texas

FIRST EDITION

I dedicate this book
to all my loved ones, my family;
to the memory of the late Charles Barrera of San Antonio,
and, of course,
to the Granaderos and the Damas de Gálvez.

Contents

Picture (1975) of Granderos de Gálvez Founders; The Hon. Erik I. Martel, Consul General of Spain, in dark uniform, and the Hon. Charles Barrera of San Antonio, Texas, in Granadero Commander uniform.

Foreword

When Charlie Barrera and I founded the Granaderos de Gálvez in 1975, the thought and hope came to our minds that books
such as this would some day be published; for the aim of this book
is to try to foster interest among American youth in a period of
American history — and of Spanish history and the history of the
Hispanic people as well, which, unfortunately, is almost totally un-
known.

The amnesia afflicting many humans is a malady that needs to
be corrected; for a person without a memory cannot function well
in society. It then becomes necessary to cure this malady — or de-
ficiency — not only on an individual basis but collectively as well.
Not recalling or not knowing the contributions of Hispanics to the
United States of America has tended to create a state of amnesia in
the minds of many Americans towards this important group of
Americans.

Fortunately, the treatment for this type of amnesia can be easily corrected — or cured — by incorporating this data in the history
textbooks on American history studied at all levels: elementary,
secondary, college, and university. This task is of great importance,
for the American people love the truth. The American people want
the *whole* truth. Furthermore, this assumes even greater importance
as the contributions of certain states, like Texas for instance, are
not properly and fully recognized. Likewise, there is a lack of justice
and objectivity in not recognizing the fact that Hispanics have had
an integral part in the development of this great nation from the
very beginning and by right have proven that they are as loyal
Americans as the Founding Fathers.

when we founded the Granaderos de Gálvez the theme of "the
contributions of Hispanics to the independence of this country" be-

came the focus as the Bicentennial of American Independence was just about to begin. We, however, set for ourselves the task of going beyond that point in time. Our aim was also to help the American public become aware and more cognizant of all areas — or aspects — of Spain's rightful place in American history, beginning with the Discovery of the Americas in 1492 and the subsequent explorations, the Christianization of the American natives, the transplantation of Spanish culture in the New World, and the beginnings of Spanish settlement in many places which now are part of the United States of America.

That was our immediate and long-range goal. Something which we hope is in the process of being realized.

ERIK I. MARTEL
Consul General of Spain
for the southeastern United States
Coral Gables, Florida
June 1991

Acknowledgments

The moral support and encouragement in the writing of this short monograph has come from many good friends of long standing. I wish, however, to recognize and thank in a special way those who have been more directly involved in this project: Dr. W. H. Timmons — professor emeritus of history at the University of Texas at El Paso; Dr. Thomas E. Chávez, Director of the Governors Palace Museum in Santa Fe, New Mexico; and Dr. Gene Alan Muller, Professor of History at El Paso Community College. I also wish to recognize Dr. Domingo Nick Reyes of La Fe Clinic in El Paso, as well as the well-known sculptor and painter, John Sherrill Houser.

Likewise, I also wish to recognize and thank my good friend and former teacher, the highly-respected historian and author, Dr. W. H. Timmons, as well as another well-known southwest historian and co-Granadero, Leon Metz.

The moral support — through their endorsements — is also deeply appreciated from: Dr. Diana Natalicio, President of the University of Texas at El Paso; Dr. Gene Alan Muller, Professor of History at El Paso Community College; the Honorable Erik Ignacio Martel, Consul General of Spain for the southeastern United States, with headquarters in Coral Gables, Florida; and of my equally good and dear friend, Dr. Miguel Ayuso Torres, Professor of Law and Legal Philosophy at Spain's National University (la Universidad Complutense de Madrid), and also at the Universidad Pontificia.

The frontispiece, General Bernardo de Gálvez on horseback, leading his troops to battle, is the work of the famous El Pasoan, José Cisneros. Mr. Cisneros, too, has been most enthusiastic in his support. The other two major illustrations, of the de Gálvez Brothers, and of the Granadero the work of my good friend John Sherrill Houser.

And, as the cliché goes, "last but not least," my gratitude to my wife Carmelita for her insistence and persistence that I write "something about Bernardo de Gálvez" geared to school-age children, that they may get to know "who Bernardo de Gálvez was and what he did."

To all of them — each and everyone — my heartfelt thanks and gratitude.

Introduction

A dedicated student and teacher of the history and culture of Spain and Spanish-America for over forty years is Lorenzo G. LaFarelle of El Paso, Texas. Educated in the schools of Texas, Mexico, and Spain, he has served as educator and counselor in the public schools of El Paso and as part-time instructor at the El Paso Community College and now at the University of Texas at El Paso. He has been recipient of many honors in his academic career, and his reputation as a dedicated servant and trusted friend to all his associates and students has long been well established.

Historian LaFarelle's primary interest for many years has been Bernardo de Gálvez, member of the illustrious family of 18th century Spanish administrators. Don Bernardo came to America in 1769, serving as frontier commander until 1777 when he was appointed governor of Spanish Louisiana. The loss of Florida to Great Britain in 1763 brought forth a Spanish anti-British policy, and the American Revolution offered Spain a great opportunity to strike back at a traditional enemy. As governor of Spanish Louisiana, therefore, de Gálvez aided the Patriot cause in two different ways — first, by providing supplies, arms, and credits to American forces fighting in the Ohio and Mississippi River valleys; and second, by launching military offensives against the British in Florida, thus preventing Britain from employing those forces against the Americans in the critical 1780–1781 period. De Gálvez' forces in 1779 took Baton Rouge and Natchez; in 1780 they took Mobile Bay, and in 1781 they forced the British to surrender at Pensacola Bay. This not only ensured the return of Florida to Spain; it also made possible the American victory over British forces at Yorktown.

Although de Gálvez' victory at Pensacola should be viewed as one of the most significant military engagements of the period, it has received scant attention from historians of the American Revolution. Thus the name of Bernardo de Gálvez, LaFarelle insists, should be placed in proper perspective as one of the unsung heroes of the American Revolution. To this end, it should be noted, an organization known as "Los Granaderos de Gálvez" was founded in 1975 by prominent civic leaders in San Antonio, Houston, Galveston, and El Paso to direct attention to the important role that de Gálvez played during the American Revolution and to ensure that he receives the honor and recognition that he deserves. Historian LaFarelle's informative biographical study should contribute significantly to the realization of that worthy and important objective.

Painting of Macharavialla, the birthplace of Bernardo de Gálvez, in the Old Governor's Mansion, Baton Rouge, Louisiana.

CHAPTER I

Macharavialla

The story we are about to unfold had its beginning in Macharavialla, a mountain village in the province of Málaga, the south central coast of Spain so popular today as a major tourist and resort attraction. The warm waters of the Mediterranean Sea bathe its shores and make its sands especially attractive to people from northern climes. Today, hundreds of thousands of visitors swarm to the Costa del Sol every year to relax on its expansive beaches and to absorb the rays of the Spanish sun.

Macharavialla is a picturesque Andalusian village on the slope of the Mountains of Málaga about 12 miles east from the port of Málaga. From a distance it resembles a multi-levelled hive because all houses and public buildings are white-washed. Flowers abound everywhere. The intense light gives its skies a vivid blue tint, while in the distance the waters of the Mediterranean acquire a bluish-green hue. The sound of the beat of the sea is heard.

All along the slopes of this mountain town are almond and fig trees, patches of locust trees, pomegranates, and an olive grove here and there. Below, in the rich soil of the ravines are lemon and orange groves, thick fields of sugar cane, and vineyards. The locally produced wines, especially the *raisin must* variety — amber and honey in color, have figured among the finest in the world. This tranquil village was the childhood environment of the central figure of our story, Bernardo de Gálvez.

It was not far from Macharavialla that the last and final battle

1

for the expulsion of the Moors from Spain took place. Northeast of Macharavialla lies the beautiful and historic and fabled city of Granada, the last of the Moorish strongholds in the Iberian peninsula. And, it was to Granada that the valiant and great Queen Isabel la Católica personally led her troops to the battle, the final battle of the Reconquest, which would free Spain, once and for all, from the Muslims. On January 2, 1492, her husband, King Fernando, received the keys to Granada from Boabdil, the son of the last Arab ruler in Spain. Spain was now to be under Christian rule.

It was precisely in the last of these wars against the Moors that a family of Spanish daring and valiant warriors by the name of *de Gálvez* became even more famous for their brave deeds. The male heirs of the de Gálvez family were knighted by the Spanish monarchs for their exploits against the Moors. The de Gálvez family was thereby inducted into the ranks of the Spanish nobility and assumed its rightful place among those who had fought long and hard to reconquer Granada, the last Moorish Kingdom. Their place in history was now assured.

It was into a family of descendants of such noble lineage and great traditions that a boy was born on July 23, 1746. The boy was baptized in the village church and was named Bernardo Vicente Polimar de Gálvez y Gallardo. Eventually he was to be known simply as Bernardo de Gálvez.

Bernardo's parents were Don Matías de Gálvez and Doña Josefa Madrid y Gallardo de Gálvez. Bernardo was their first born.

The de Gálvez Brothers: Matías and José. Don Matías on the left, Don José on the right, by John S. Houser, 1991.

CHAPTER II

The de Gálvez Brothers

Bernardo's family had long distinguished itself in the royal service of Spain. His father, Don Matías de Gálvez, after serving as Captain-General of Guatemala, was elevated to Viceroy of New Spain, 1783–84. His uncle, José, was appointed Minister of the Indies, and exercised power second only to King Carlos III himself. Another uncle, Miguel, was a Field Marshal in the Ejército Real de España, the Spanish Royal Army. A third uncle, Antonio, served as Spanish Ambassador to the Czar of Russia.

Bernardo's favorite uncle, José, one of the mentors he was fortunate to have, was a brilliant attorney. José's fame and prestige had grown so, we are told, that he even dared to represent a foreign firm engaged in litigation with the Crown. Unhappy with his action the King called him and asked for an explanation; whereupon, José's reply to his Majesty was: "Sire, before the King there is the law." It was Uncle José who was to lay the groundwork, the plan for the foundings of San Diego, San Buenaventura, Monterey and San Francisco, in present-day California, and eventually even the explorations of the coast of far-away Alaska as far north as Point Valdez, in an effort to halt the possible Russian encroachment into that part of North America.

Another of Uncle José's accomplishments after his visitation of New Spain, between the years of 1765–71, was to prevail upon the powerful Council of the Indies to effect a new reorganization of the Viceroyalty of New Spain, creating in the process the so-called In-

4

The other two de Gálvez Brothers: Antonio and Miguel. Antonio on the left, Miguel on the right, by John S. Houser, 1991.

terior Provinces: New Vizcaya, Sinaloa, Sonora, Coahuila, the two Californias — upper and lower, New Mexico and Texas. The Comandancia General for New Mexico and Texas was to be established in the city of Chihuahua, "with the very important aim" and these are his words, "of giving spirit and movement to such vast territories, naturally rich, which in a few years may form an empire equal to or greater than this in Mexico."

On the cultural level, Don José was the founder of the Archive of the Indies, a specialized collection of books, maps and writings on Indian affairs. His Archive in Sevilla is universally used today as a primary source for research by scholars from around the world.

Bernardo's father, Matías, was himself a man of achievement. He went into the Army, reviving the military vocation of the de Gálvez family in previous centuries. From ensign he rose to Captain-General. His first command was in the Canary Islands. In 1778 he was named Captain-General and President of the Royal Audience of Guatemala. With the declaration of war between Spain and Great Britain, Matías led his troops in several important engagements against the British in Guatemala, Nicaragua, and in Honduras.

By the year 1780 the de Gálvez brothers: Matías, José, Antonio, and Miguel, although in different settings and in different fields, were all at the zenith of their glory and power. For his successes in Central America, Bernardo's father, Matías, would soon be named Viceroy of New Spain. Bernardo's mentor, his Uncle José, was at the height of his influence in the government as the King's personal advisor. Antonio had reached the rank of Field Marshal, the highest in the Army and a much decorated officer. Miguel was Minister of the Council of War, President of the Royal Academy of Law, Mayor of the Imperial Household and Court, Governor, and member of innumerable Boards and Councils.

And now there was a fifth de Gálvez, Bernardo, the son of Matías.

CHAPTER III

Bernardo

Bernardo, following his father's example, chose the military profession at an early age. A cadet in the Military Academy of Avila, at the age of sixteen he enlisted as a volunteer in the war with Portugal and fought there as an infantry lieutenant.

In 1765, coinciding with Uncle José's visitation of New Spain, Bernardo embarked for Mexico, accompanying his uncle. He was commissioned as captain in the army of General Don Juan de Villalva, and, in 1769, assigned to the army of la Nueva Vizcaya (the present Mexican state of Chihuahua and Southwest Texas). The headquarters of the command was in the city of Chihuahua. Bernardo soon replaced Don Lope de Cuéllar as military commander, for Viceroy Croix determined to entrust him with the pacification of the warlike Apaches, Mescaleros and Lipanes. Bernardo was twenty-four years old at the time he was made military commander of la Nueva Vizcaya and Sonora.

He fought the Opata Indians and made an effective treaty with them whereby the Opatas recognized him as their Chief and obligated themselves to fight the unfriendly Indian nations, one of which was the much feared Apaches. The Apaches spread destruction through all the region of the North and raised a seemingly insurmountable obstacle to Spanish colonization of that territory.

In 1770–71, Bernardo led several successful expeditions against the Apaches in northern Chihuahua and Southwest Texas. With a troop of 200 men he marched through inhospitable deserts

7

from the city of Chihuahua to the Pecos River; his men oftentimes hungry and thirsty, and demoralized. He, however, so inspired them with his example, courage, valor, and his words of encouragement, that they swore that "they would follow him to the death."

Bernardo was wounded on several occasions; on the last of these he was carried off with two spear wounds in the chest and an arrow in his left arm. In the last major battle Bernardo took several prisoners and in 1771, when he returned to Mexico City, he escorted fourteen young Apache braves whom he enrolled in the Franciscan Colegio de San Gregorio. War, for Bernardo, did not mean the extermination of the conquered.

The experience he gained fighting Indians in Chihuahua and Southwest Texas was to prove invaluable and useful in the actions he would have to face later in the Mississippi Valley, fighting powerful Indian nations allied with the English. His experiences in Chihuahua and Texas gave him a good insight into the character, customs, and laws of the Indian people. This proved an asset later, while governor and military commander of the province of Louisiana.

In 1771, after his last two major successful expeditions against the Apaches, Viceroy Croix recommended Bernardo's promotion to Lieutenant Colonel. This was quickly approved. Upon his return to Mexico City in early 1772, at his Uncle José's invitation and with the Viceroy's approval, Bernardo returned to Spain, once again accompanying his uncle, the Visitador de las Indias.

After his arrival in Spain and once at Court, Bernardo asked and received permission to go to France to undertake further studies to perfect himself in the art and science of warfare. He enrolled in the Regiment of Cantabria and spent three years there, attaining the rank of Lieutenant in that elite corps. Besides broadening his military expertise, his stay in France facilitated his learning of the French language and culture, which had a great bearing on his future military and political career in Louisiana. The French Louisianans were greatly impressed with Bernardo's knowledge of their language and culture. And, needless to say, this made him instantly popular in Louisiana after his arrival there in 1776.

Eventually, Bernardo married a beautiful and vivacious young lady of the New Orleans French high society, Marie Felicité de Saint-Maxent. Marie Felicité, quoting from reports of those days, was "as beautiful as she was charming, and loved by all." She was the widow of Don Juan Bautista d'Estrehan, by whom she had a daughter, Adelaida. Marie Felicité was the daughter of Don Gilberto Antonio de Saint-Maxent, a prominent businessman and financier of Louisiana. For his outstanding loyalty and service to the cause of Spain in Louisiana, Don Gilberto, with the consent and approval of Carlos III was named Captain of the Militia Infantry of New Orleans. The chronicles of the time also say that Marie Felicité and Bernardo had a "romantic idyll" going throughout their marriage. They had three children: Matilde, Miguel, and Guadalupe; the last, Guadalupe, having been born in Mexico City just a few weeks after Bernardo's death.

Also quoting from other chronicles of the time: "Bernardo was to be the second of three Spanish governors, consecutively, to marry beautiful French creoles from New Orleans." Many other Spanish officers did likewise; undoubtedly, among other reasons, to gain social acceptability.

In 1775 Bernardo returned to Spain from France and was incorporated into the Infantry Regiment of Sevilla. He participated in the ill-fated attack on Algiers, taking part both in the landing and the assault on the fortress. He was wounded a third time. Again, his conduct was heroic. He refused to be carried from the battlefield until he saw the Spanish banner waving over the fortress of Algiers. For his valor and merits of war Bernardo was promoted once again. After convalescence, he was assigned to the Military Academy in Avila, which he had left years before as a cadet. Now Bernardo returned to educate and train other aspirants in the art and science of warfare, further enriching this by his own field experience. But he soon received a call, another call from the Court. His Majesty, at the proposal and recommendation of the Royal Council, decided to send him to New Orleans as head of the Fixed Garrison Regiment. His Majesty decided that he wanted "to have a person of *my* complete confidence in that important place." And, Bernardo was that person, that man, that soldier.

Portrait of Don Bernardo de Gálvez, a painting from his period as Governor of Louisiana, Old Governor's Mansion, Baton Rouge, Louisiana.

11

CHAPTER IV

Bernardo in Louisiana

In mid-1776 Bernardo was transferred to the faraway Province of Louisiana as Colonel of the Louisiana Regiment. Bernardo arrived in the city of New Orleans, capital of the province, and immediately presented himself — and his letters of commission from Captain-General Don Alejandro O'Reilly, Field Marshal and Supreme Commander of the Spanish Army — to Governor Don Luis de Unzaga. After the formalities called forth by protocol, he assumed command of his regiment.

On January 1, 1777, a royal order named Bernardo acting governor of the vast province which had quite suddenly, because of its strategic location and its proximity to the American colonies which were now waging war against Great Britain for their independence, acquired a tremendous importance. For, was not New Orleans also the gateway to the important and navigable Mississippi River?

The vast province of Louisiana had been named in honor of King Louis XIV of France by Robert Cavelier, Sieur de La Salle, who claimed it for France in 1682. French settlements soon followed. It had been ceded by France to Spain in 1763, at the end of the Seven Year War, also known as the French and Indian War, in compensation for the loss of Florida to England, according to the terms of the Paris Peace Treaty ending said war. The immense Louisiana territory extended almost all the way from the river's mouth to the region of the Great Lakes on the border with Canada.

The population was sparse, limited to French colonists who for the most part engaged in the cultivation of rice, tobacco, indigo, and cotton, and, preferably, in the trade of skins. A chain of small French military outposts along the Mississippi guaranteed the navigation of the river and trade with the Indian nations who lived in the great forests. And at the mouth of the river, of course, was New Orleans, a city with personality and style; a city which imitated the fashions and customs of the French Court at Versailles and, later, the Spanish Court at Madrid. The city of New Orleans had grown in importance as a center of trade, commerce, and culture. Under the Spanish, the city continued to grow even more and to prosper and to acquire a definite Latin ambience. Even today, New Orleans preserves a marked and unmistakable Latin atmosphere. When people think of New Orleans they think of France in America.

During the forty years of Spanish rule — 1763–1803 — Louisiana flourished. The population grew from 10,000 to 50,000. Bernardo and his successors promoted immigration and brought groups of Spanish colonists who transformed great expanses of virgin land into fertile farms and plantations. In 1778, 1,582 immigrants from the Canary Islands arrived. These Canary Islanders founded several important settlements on the banks of the Mississippi: *Valenzuela, Tierra del Buey,* and *Barataria.* In 1779, another 500 settlers, countrymen of Bernardo, arrived from Málaga. These Málagans founded New Iberia. Each family was generously provided with a house, cattle, fowl, tools and farm implements, and a food ration for four years. American refugees and settlers also came. They built a town to the Northwest of New Orleans and named it Galveztown, in honor of Bernardo. Another town founded by American refugees was New Feliciana; so named in honor of Bernardo's wife.

In his capacity as Governor of Louisiana from 1777 to 1783, Bernardo showed his ability as a man of state. He initiated measures that were to be proven effective in the course of his administration of that immense territory. He provided for its defense, population growth, and of course, good administration. His primary mission was to guarantee the security of the Spanish domains bordering on the Mississippi and the Gulf Coast. Under him, Louisiana also became a haven to both English and American refugees. He interpreted liberally the commercial regulations he as governor was supposed to enforce, those pertinent to trade between the

Spanish colonies and the French colonies. He did, however, curtail the contraband trade of the English merchants. And, while there was a lively trade in skins, he made the expansion of agriculture one of his primary objectives.

In his vision and resourcefulness, Bernardo saw the need for the growth of population as the basic condition for promoting the economic and commercial development of the province.

The consideration, respect, and recognition he always extended to those who helped him, without distinction of rank or race was, without doubt, a determining factor in the loyalty he always received from those who were associated with him in his endeavors. He was a popular governor, well-liked and respected. His command of the French language and his knowledge of French ways and customs enabled him to work effectively with the French Louisianans.

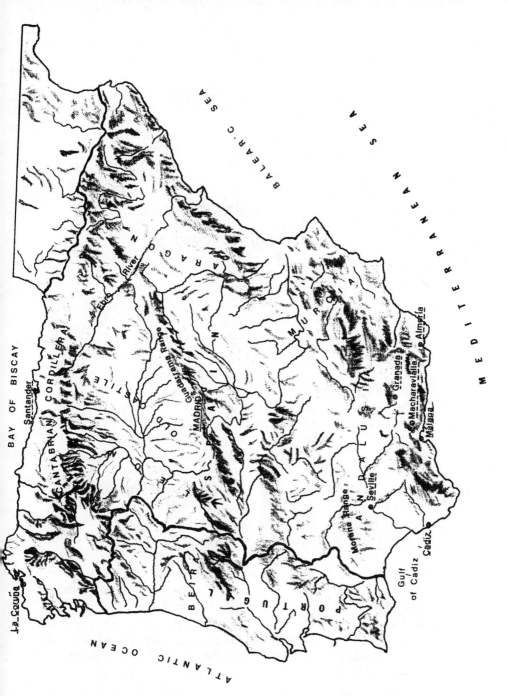

Map of Spain and Portugal, showing sites in Spain mentioned in the story, by Abel Ramírez of EPCC, El Paso, Texas, 1991.

15

CHAPTER V

Spain's Assistance to the Americans

As Governor of Louisiana, Bernardo had received instructions from the Spanish Crown to give secret assistance to the American rebels in their War of Independence, also often referred to as the American Revolution.

After the French and Indian War of 1757–1763, the American colonists had been growing progressively restless under British rule, which they felt oppressive and arbitrary. The British imperial system, based on the policy of mercantilism, the Americans felt especially hurtful to their economic interests. Furthermore, there was the issue — among others — of "taxation without representation." The Americans had tried open discussion with the British Crown and the Parliament, without results. Their first armed confrontation with the British authorities occurred on the afternoon of March 5, 1770, resulting in what has been known since as the "Boston Massacre." A second armed confrontation took place in the morning of April 19, 1775, when British soldiers from Boston, under orders from General Gage to seize rebel arms and supplies supposedly stored in Concord, were met by an assortment of ill-trained farmers, a volunteer militia composed of young and old men and even boys, who decided to intercept the British regulars at Lexington. No one planned to fight, but in the confusion someone — probably a colonist — fired a shot. The redcoats responded by discharging a volley, and eight Americans lay dead. This first shot, in all probability fired accidentally by an American colonist, was to become known as "the shot heard round the world"; meaning, of course, the beginning of the American Revolution, the American War of Independence.

There was a long history of animosity and rivalry between the Spanish and the English, going as far back as the early 1530s. The divorce of King Henry VIII from Catherine of Aragón, aunt of Charles V, Holy Roman emperor and king of Spain, had triggered this. Later, in 1588, the episode of the Invincible Spanish Armada further reinforced this bad feeling. And after all these, the more recent and continuous rivalry between the two powers for control of the New World exacerbated the feelings of hostility between the two nations even more. The growth of England's maritime power threatened Spain's colonial empire. King Carlos III, in an effort to balance — or counterbalance — England's power, was forced by circumstances to ally himself with France. Carlos III's foreign policy thus came to revolve around the Family Pact, an alliance between France and Spain, which committed Spain to endless wars at sea. Thus it was that in the Peace of Paris of 1763, ending the Seven Years' War between the French and the English, that Great Britain was given possession of all land east of the Mississippi River, including Spanish Florida. Spain, in turn, was given the city of New Orleans and all of French Louisiana west of the Mississippi. Hence, French Louisiana became Spanish Louisiana.

Now, with the outbreak of hostilities between the American colonists and the Mother Country, England, came the opportunity King Carlos III of Spain had been hoping and waiting for. Carlos III felt this was his chance to win back Florida.

And, while all this was going on, Bernardo, as Governor of Louisiana, had to blend skill with audacity to carry out his orders and objectives of providing assistance to the American rebels, as Spain was not yet at war with Great Britain. He had to officially maintain an attitude of neutrality in the Anglo-American conflict. Bernardo knew, and the English did, too, that armed conflict between two powerful neighbors with opposing interests was inevitable.

Bernardo immersed himself in intense activity. He inspected, reorganized, and strengthened the Spanish military detachments along the Mississippi, made maps of the whole course of the river and of the coast, and took action against illegal trade and contraband by the British. He also made important contacts with several Indian nations and entered into treaties with them.

Among his first measures as Governor, Bernardo declared the port of New Orleans open and free to American trade. He also opted to admit and to sell the prizes of war taken by the American rebels and privateers. Spanish harbors thus became a refuge for American ships.

In April 1777, Bernardo, wishing to suppress all trade with the English, captured eleven English ships as reprisal for the capture of three Spanish merchantmen by the British. He decreed that all English subjects must leave Louisiana within fifteen days. These actions of Bernardo demonstrated to the Americans that in Bernardo they had an important and decisive ally.

In the process of assisting the American cause, Bernardo had the loyal collaboration of an Irishman, Oliver Pollock, a resident of New Orleans who had aligned himself with the American cause and soon would be named the official agent of the Virginia Legislature. Pollock had become one of the most prosperous merchants in Louisiana. He engaged in the trade of hides and furs, flour, coffee, sugar, wood, indigo, and spices and had the concession of supplying flour to the Spanish military detachments along the Mississippi. He was held in high regard by the Spanish government and the business community and considered the most solid financier in the region.

Shortly before the arrival of Bernardo in New Orleans in 1776, General Charles Lee of Williamsburg, Virginia, had asked for help by the Spanish "in the name of humanity." In his message to Governor Don Luis de Unzaga, General Lee asked for a shipment of gunpowder, medicines — particularly quinine, and food to remedy the desperate situation of Colonel Morgan at Fort Pitt (now Pittsburgh, Pennsylvania). At great personal risk as Spain was still officially neutral, Governor Unzaga ordered the aid given to the Americans through the offices of Oliver Pollock. Oliver Pollock took charge of the operation, chartered a boat and contracted with Governor Unzaga for the purchase of 10,000 pounds of gunpowder from the Spanish government stores in New Orleans. Under American Lieutenant Linn the precious cargo went up river, the boatmen rowing day and night. On May 2, 1777, the cargo arrived at Fort Pitt and the fort was saved, thanks to the assistance from the Spanish authorities in New Orleans.

Colonel Morgan, commander of Fort Pitt, wrote to Bernardo — who had now replaced Governor Unzaga — expressing his gratitude. Working closely on the project, Bernardo and Oliver Pollock later perfected a supply system from the Spanish to the American forces that functioned effectively. And, although Pollock used his own economic resources to finance these early expeditions, Bernardo oftentimes extended generous amounts of credit for this purpose. In 1777, Bernardo extended a credit of $74,078 to Pollock. One shipment worth 25,000 gold doubloons, made up of quinine, shoes, blankets, tents, and other war materiel, was sent directly from the Spanish government warehouses in New Orleans up river, routed to the American forces. The boats sailed up the Mississippi under the Spanish flag, loaded with all types of supplies: uniforms, shoes, blankets, food, medicines, lead, gunpowder, muskets, cannon and other war materiel, and money, bound for the American detachments in the upper Mississippi and to the frontiers of Virginia and Pennsylvania, from where the supplies were sent to General George Washington's army and to the southern division of General Charles Lee.

King Carlos III advanced a secret loan of 1,000,000 pounds to the Americans. For the facade of neutrality Spain wanted to project at this time, these transactions were given the character of private commercial operations. Eventually, because of the critical financial condition of the Americans, the responsibility for additional supplies fell on the Governor of Louisiana and his collaborator, Oliver Pollock. Pollock who had completely sacrificed his personal fortune, even to the point of selling his properties and being at the mercy of his creditors, was put in prison. But his good friend Bernardo came to his rescue. Bernardo himself had to answer for the debts from his personal holdings.

In 1778, up river, the English decided to attack the Spanish garrison at Fort St. Louis, about nine miles below the confluence of the Mississippi and Missouri. The Spanish military and the French colonists put up a desperate resistance to the forces of English General Sinclair, who was then compelled to call off his attack. Later, to protect St. Louis from the North, Commander Francisco Cruzat, in command at Fort St. Louis, ordered Captain Pourré to attack the English detachment at St. Joseph on Lake Michigan. St. Joseph was taken by surprise, its small garrison made prisoner and the booty was distributed among the Indians.

In the matter of assistance provided by Spain to the American rebels, we need also to mention the rich Bilbao merchant, Don

Diego de Gardoqui. Gardoqui was another very important media-
tor between the Americans and the Spanish authorities at this time.
Gardoqui would later become the first Spanish diplomat ac-
credited to the United States after independence. In 1777, according to the Spanish author and authority on Bernardo de Gálvez,
José Rodulfo Boeta, King Carlos III approved four million reales
in bullion for the Americans, which was to be used for the purchase
of "216 bronze cannon, 209 gun-carriages, 27 mortars, 12,000
bombs, 51,000 cannon balls, 300 lots of a thousand pounds of powder, 30,000 rifles with bayonets, 4,000 tents, 30,000 uniforms, and
lead for fire balls."

These supplies left from French ports and were sent to the
American rebels, via Bermuda. Regular shipments of clothing,
powder and munitions, medicines, and food, stored in the Havana
warehouses, were to be placed at the disposal of the Americans, according to instructions given to Arthur Lee, negotiator for the Continental Congress, by the Marquis of Grimaldi, representing King
Carlos III and Don Diego de Gardoqui, the commercial agent of
the firm "Gardoqui e Hijos."

Supplies destined for the Americans also left from the Spanish
ports of La Coruña, Barcelona, and Cádiz. It was Don Diego de
Gardoqui who was in charge of organizing the financial and commercial channels for these "exports," by obtaining substantial
credits for the Americans from the Spanish Crown. In addition to
the supplies already shipped to the Americans and mentioned
above, the following credits were extended to the Americans: "In
1777, in the month of March, 3,000 pesos; 50,000 pesos in April; in
April, also 8,100 pounds and, in June, 106,000 in other currency";
all according to José Rodulfo Boeta in his book *Bernardo de Gálvez*.
Also, according to Boeta, late in December 1777, the Americans
asked Spain for another loan of "two million pounds sterling."

According to Professor Yela Utrilla in the book, *Spain and the
Independence of the United States,* included in a "Complete Record of
Supplies and costs before September 1777, catalogued in the National Historic Archive in Madrid, File No. 3,884, are detailed,
item by item, the acquisitions made by the American Commission-
ers charged to the credits conceded in Spain to Arthur Lee, to the
sum of 7,730,000 pounds." And this was just the beginning. Thus
we can safely and accurately say according to the American historian, Helen Auger, that "Spain shod and dressed the American sol-

diers, armed their units with the Spanish musket of 1757, then considered the best in the world, supplied with powder and cannon their magazines and artillery and even built and equipped the ships to transport the goods." Helen Auger, an expert and authority on this period in American history, has with reason said that "this aid was of great importance to a country that was as naked and defenseless as an oyster shell."

In the meantime, Bernardo was communicating with the Americans Patrick Henry and General Charles Lee, both of Virginia. Benjamin Franklin was also communicating with the Count of Aranda, a high Minister of State and Spain's Secretary of Foreign Affairs. In one of his letters, Franklin thanked the Count of Aranda effusively for the 12,000 muskets sent to Boston by Spain. Thomas Jefferson also expressed appreciation for Spain's aid in a letter to Bernardo dated November 8, 1779.

Adding to what I have already said and quoted above on the matter of Spain's assistance to the American rebels, I want to close this chapter by quoting two other well-known contemporary Americans, the late famous TV personality and author, Catholic Bishop Fulton J. Sheen, and the Honorable Stanton Griffiths, highly respected Ambassador of the United States to Spain after World War II. Bishop Sheen said, and these are his words: "Spain was our friend from the beginning, even before independence was declared. Spain allowed our ships to enter all her ports. The king of Spain gave us $5,000,000 dollars in support of our cause." Ambassador Griffiths, in 1952, had this to say: "Why American historians have always tried to hide, or at least to play down, all the help Spain gave us at the moment of independence, while praising French aid, is beyond my comprehension. They even overlook the fact that Carlos III gave the Americans their first loan so as to buy uniforms, munitions and items for its shirtless army. During fifteen years Spain paid, punctually, one after the other, in the banks of Austria, Germany, and Holland, notes which the United States could not honor."

CHAPTER VI

Bernardo and George Rogers Clark

George Rogers Clark, who in the early 1800s was to gain fame for his exploration of the Louisiana Territory shortly after its acquisition from France by President Thomas Jefferson, was a man who was also very much involved in the American War of Independence. As a military leader on the American western frontier, George Rogers Clark had already gained fame during the American Revolution for his daring and dramatic expedition from Kentucky into the Illinois territory. After organizing and leading Kentucky militiamen in the defense of their settlements, Clark decided to carry the war to the British by attacking posts in Illinois. With fewer than 200 men, he took Kaskaskia without resistance in July 1778. Clark's success in this action convinced the French inhabitants of Cahokia and Vincennes to join with him.

In the meantime, the British commander at Detroit, Henry Hamilton, took the offensive against the French at Vincennes and in December 1778 captured it. Two months later, however, Clark led a small force across the harsh winter terrain, retook Vincennes and captured Hamilton. This, among other military actions, made George Rogers Clark widely known and acclaimed. The attack and recapture of Vincennes was the high point in Clark's career.

Clark had of course already heard of the Spanish help that had made possible for the Americans to remain in control of Fort Pitt. Through the grapevine, Clark had heard how Colonel Morgan, commander of Fort Pitt, had promptly acknowledged the Spanish aid that had made this possible in a letter to Bernardo in May 1777. Now, George Rogers Clark also began to seek aid from the Spanish governor in New Orleans, Bernardo de Gálvez. Clark's petition to Bernardo was one of a flood of petitions from the Americans asking de Gálvez for aid of every kind.

It is in this connection that Clark and Bernardo established a relationship that was to link the two throughout the war and beyond. This close friendly relationship between Bernardo and Clark brought other famous American fighters into contact with Bernardo, the legendary Daniel Boone, James Harrod, and Benjamin Logan.

Clark's campaigns along the Illinois had served as a check against the plots concocted by the British commander in Detroit, who, with great resources in money, arms, provisions, and gifts, had mobilized a powerful mercenary army of several thousand powerful Indians from the warlike tribes of those areas against the American settlers then living in those remote outposts.

English commander Hamilton's objective was to attack Kentucky and close the Ohio River to possible Spanish aid from New Orleans. Clark, aware of the seriousness of Hamilton's plan, decided to thwart Hamilton's plans by taking the offensive and capturing the English detachments on the Illinois. Once he had taken Kaskaskia, Vincennes and other forts, Clark would then take and occupy Detroit. Thus he would realize his dream of the American occupation of the then Northwest territory.

Clark presented his plan to the Congress of Virginia and urgently requested men, arms, provisions, and money for his undertaking. Virginia, however, like the rest of the colonies, was unable to finance Clark's project. Clark's only recourse now was to turn South, to the port city of New Orleans, capital of Spanish Louisiana. There, he had heard, was a man who would help him, Governor Bernardo de Gálvez, assisted, of course, in his endeavors by his loyal friend and collaborator, the Irish merchant Oliver Pollock. Bernardo responded to Clark's request to the fullest extent of his ability. Without hesitation he used completely the funds he had available for the maintenance of his province, Louisiana. Oliver Pollock, likewise, did the same; sacrificing his personal fortune to the extent of selling his properties.

In the meantime, English General Sinclair organized an expedition to conquer Illinois and St. Louis. The English were assisted in this by a contingent of Sioux warriors led by the famous Wabasha, the most feared Indian in the territory. General Sinclair's column was to attack the Spanish fort at St. Louis. St. Louis was of great importance because of its strategic location, as well as for its economic and trade value, being as it was the center of the fur trade in the Mississippi Valley.

The Spanish commander of the fort at St. Louis was Fernando de Leyba, a close associate of Bernardo's and one in whom Bernardo had total confidence. De Leyba had a tiny garrison under his command, composed, as he said in his letter to Bernardo, "of sixteen men, including the drummer boy." St. Louis, however, was soon reinforced by 300 colonists and merchants of the city, as well as by a small contingent from Fort Santa Genoveva.

Among the volunteers was Francisco Vigo, an old retired Spanish colonel now dedicated to the fur trade. On seeing so much determination and resistance on the part of the Spanish, General Sinclair called off his attack.

After this incident and a short time later, Clark, helped by the generous supplies he had received from Bernardo and Oliver Pollock, began his counteroffensive. In the meantime, Commander de Leyba had also provided a hundred reinforcements to Clark. Thus, Clark was able, after a terrible march, to fall by surprise on the English forts at Kaskaskia, Cahokia, and Vincennes, and capture them. This enabled Clark to dominate the region and thus frustrate the English designs. In this way Clark was able to maintain control of the territories west of the Allegheny Mountains.

Not long afterward, the Spanish commander at Fort St. Louis, Cruzat, ordered a small expedition of Spanish soldiers and friendly Indians under Captain Pourré against the English detachment at San José on Lake Michigan. San José was taken by surprise, its garrison made prisoner and the booty distributed among the Indians.

After this, the Mississippi River, from its source to its mouth on the Gulf coast was free of British interference. Bernardo had, to a great extent, made this possible by his generous assistance to George Rogers Clark and that of his associate, Commander de Leyba.

CHAPTER VII

Preparing for War

News and messages Bernardo received in the summer of 1779 all coincided. The English were preparing for an invasion of Louisiana and a major attack on New Orleans. They were massing their forces in Canada and in Florida with this objective and to achieve definite control of the valley of the Mississippi. In this way they also would be able to strangle the American rebellion which in good part was staying alive through the Spanish assistance it was receiving.

Bernardo, faced with the intelligence he was receiving and with the urgency required because of the impending situation, called a meeting of his Military Council. All the military commanders and "jefes políticos" of the forts and districts in the Mississippi Valley and the frontier with Florida attended. Even the military commander of the far-away Fort of St. Louis in the territory of Missouri, Commander Cruzat, was present.

Bernardo reported on the messages to the English garrisons which had been intercepted, as well as on information from other sources, which confirmed British military plans. His own intelligence confirmed the English preparations, their state of alertness and overall preparedness. All indicated an imminent outbreak of hostilities as well as the fact that 400 German Waldeck soldiers had reinforced the English fort at Manchak.

In addition to all these preliminaries the British had enlisted the Iroquois and Sioux Indians as allies for a full offensive against New Orleans.

25

It was decided in Council to concentrate in New Orleans all the soldiers and means of defense available and, in the meantime, to ask for urgent help from Havana in Cuba. Misfortune, however, beset Bernardo, for a highly destructive hurricane swept across the the region a few days later and sank all the boats in the Mississippi.

While all this was happening, Bernardo received dispatches from the Captain General of Cuba informing him of the declaration of war between Spain and England. Spain formally declared war against Great Britain on May 8, 1779. Secretly, Bernardo had already been recruiting men and collecting guns and supplies "for the defense of Louisiana."

Bernardo withheld the information from the official dispatch he had received from the Captain General of Cuba temporarily, possibly to better prepare his plans for action. Then Bernardo decided to call together the whole population of New Orleans in a great public assembly to tell them that Spain had been declared an enemy by England "as a consequence of the recognition of American independence." He proceeded to tell them of the declaration of war by Spain against England. He also explained the weakness of the forces of Louisiana in comparison to the English. Next, he told the people in his forceful and eloquent oratory: "I will defend the province. I am ready to shed the last drop of my blood for Louisiana and for my King." He, however, cautioned them that he could not do this alone unless they approved of his action and promised to help him "resist the ambitious designs of the British." The reaction was unanimous and overwhelming. The whole population of the city spoke with one voice, in the affirmative; they were behind him. The people authorized him to: "Take the oath; for the defense of Louisiana and in the service of the King, for we offer you our lives and our fortunes." having thus achieved the adhesion of the people, Bernardo decided to move fast; he speeded up his preparations.

Against the advice of some of his officers to remain on the defensive, Bernardo decided to take the offensive. He decided to launch a series of lightning-fast attacks on the British forts on the Mississippi. Moving before the enemy was the only card he had to play. Four boats were raised from the riverbed and equipped with ten cannon which defended New Orleans. Other ships were requisitioned along the coast. Bernardo secured the access to the Mississippi River and made doubly sure that the lifeline to the American forces remained open to them.

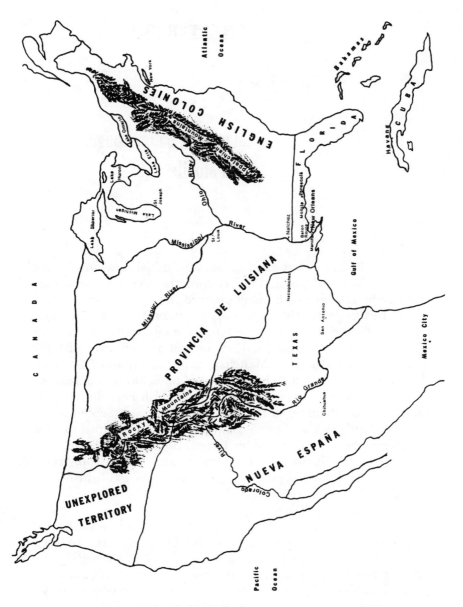

Map of what later became the United States of America showing the English Colonies, the Province of Louisiana, and New Spain. Battle sites are shown on map. By Abel Ramírez of EPCC, El Paso, Texas, 1991.

CHAPTER VIII

Manchak, Baton Rouge, and Mobile

Once Bernardo was satisfied with his initial measures for the defense of New Orleans and for securing the access to the Mississippi, he proceeded with his long-planned strategy for a swift attack on the British posts. Although ready to attack Fort Butte at Manchak immediately, a devastating hurricane forced him to delay his plans. Finally, on August 27, 1779, he and a small army of 1,472 men left New Orleans for Manchak, about ninety miles up-river. After a very difficult march through the thick forest and swampy terrain they had to cross, Bernardo took British Fort Butte by assault. The commander of the fort surrendered on September 7, 1779, and although not a major battle, the victory helped to raise the morale and confidence of his troops. Besides, Fort Butte, situated at the confluence of the Iberville and Mississippi rivers marked the boundary between Spanish Louisiana and British West Florida. After a few days' rest, Bernardo and his men marched from there to Baton Rouge.

The British fort at Baton Rouge was well-built and defended by a moat with eighteen cannon and about 600 defenders. In order to save lives, Bernardo decided against an assault. Instead, he decided to move at night and, as a diversionary tactic, sent a detachment into a wooded area near the fort. While this drew the enemy's attention and gunfire, Bernardo quietly moved his artillery into position. When the British discovered Bernardo's strategy, it was too late for them to do anything about it. On September 21, the Louisiana troops began firing, and three hours after the start of the attack Colonel Dickson and 600 men under him surrendered. In the articles of capitulation, Bernardo demanded the surrender of Fort Pan Mure in Natchez along with Baton Rouge. The British commander acceded to Bernardo's demands. On October 25, the Spanish took possession of Fort Pan Mure from British Captain Forster. This victory swept the British from the Mississippi, and Bernardo was rewarded with a promotion to Brigadier General.

General Bernardo de Gálvez now looked to the east. There was Fort Charlotte in Mobile and some distance to the southeast of Mobile there was Pensacola in British West Florida, right by the Gulf of Mexico. Pensacola was indeed a prize as it was a coveted harbor. Furthermore, General de Gálvez felt it was his soldierly duty to retake possession of Pensacola for Spain and his King.

After asking for troops from Cuba, General de Gálvez led a landing force of about 750 Spaniards, French Creoles, free men of color, and slaves aboard a twelve ship fleet into Mobile Bay. Eventually, after the arrival of reinforcements, his force was to comprise 1,400 men. Following a brief siege of Fort Charlotte in Mobile, British Commander Durnford surrendered to General de Gálvez on August 14, 1780. Immediately afterward the English flag was lowered and the Spanish flag was raised over Fort Charlotte.

In his strategy, General de Gálvez had felt it important to concentrate on Mobile before proceeding to Pensacola. Again, he had relied heavily on artillery emplacements on a trench dug close to the fort. His artillery had been so effective in battering the fort, beginning in the morning of March 12th, that Captain Durnford offered to surrender early in the evening of the same day. The next day was spent in drawing up the articles of capitulation and, on the following day, March 14th, the surrender of the British to the Spanish became official.

Once again, because of his merits and victories, General de Gálvez was promoted; this time to Field Marshal, the highest of all ranks in the Army. Furthermore, he was now given command of all Spanish operations in the Americas.

After all these victories Field Marshal Bernardo de Gálvez now had as his major immediate objective, Pensacola, in British West Florida. He even sensed that this might be the climax of his career. He prepared for it. The first three British forts captured were just the beginning of his Gulf Coast campaign. His real objective, overall, was the complete expulsion of the English from the Mississippi River and the Gulf of Mexico.

ENGLISH SOLDIER   GERMAN SOLDIER

WILLIAM McINTOSH, CREEK LEADER

The English, German, and Indian Defenders of Fort St. George in Pensacola. From Barrancas Bugle, *Gálvez Commission, Pensacola, 1981.*

31

CHAPTER IX

On to Pensacola

The stage was now set for the principal objective on the Gulf Coast: the conquest of Pensacola, the capital of British West Florida. Florida held many fond memories for the Spaniards. They were the first Europeans to explore it in 1513, and colonize it soon thereafter. Ponce de León gave Florida its Spanish name. San Agustín de la Florida was the first North American city. It was in Florida that the first Catholic Mass in continental North America had been celebrated by a Spanish Franciscan priest, Father Francisco López de Mendoza. The Franciscan Friars — first Catholic missionaries to the New World — had built a string of thirty-four missions along the coast, from San Agustín to Catalina Island, off the coast of Georgia. Yes, Florida had been Spanish and it must be Spanish again.

Before undertaking the siege and eventual capture of the city and coveted harbor and well-protected bay of Pensacola, General de Gálvez, realizing his army's weakness, embarked for Cuba to seek support for his strategy. In October 1780 he departed from Havana with a fleet and close to 4,000 men. A strong hurricane, however, widely scattered the ships far from their destination and compelled him to return to Havana. Eventually, he was able to muster another small force of 1,315 men and sent orders to New Orleans and Mobile for their forces to converge on Pensacola. Finally, on February 28, 1781, he set out once again from Havana to Pensacola, the twenty transports carrying his troops convoyed by the warship *San Ramón,* the frigates *Santa Clara* and *Caimán,* and the packet-boat *San Gil.* To all these vessels must be added the four vessels from Louisiana, among them the felucca *Valenzuela* and the barkentine *Galveztown.* General de Gálvez embarked in the warship of the line *San Ramón* and, to avoid discord, assumed complete command of the expedition. This, however, was short-lived, for there soon appeared friction and disagreements among the naval commanders themselves, and towards him.

Pensacola was well-fortified and defended by the Castle of St. George and the artillery of the Fort Barrancas Coloradas. On the Island of Santa Rosa, which fronted Pensacola Bay, an old blockhouse guarded the entrance to the bay and its artillery, despite its distant position, held the entrance channel within range. Across the channel from Santa Rosa Island, on the opposite side, and in what the British called Tartar Point was a blockhouse that guarded the west entrance to the bay. Some 1,200 yards north of the old Spanish Plaza de Pensacola was situated a hill named Gage Hill by the English. Gage Hill extended northwestward from the plaza. It was on the southeast of Gage Hill that the British built Fort George.

Fort George, according to descriptions we have, was 1,000 feet long — east to west — and 750 feet north to south. As part of fortifications there was, of course, the inevitable stockade — "measuring 1,400 feet east to west and 850 feet north to south"; the Fort itself being 1,000 feet long at the shoreline and some 750 feet north from the water's edge. Gage Hill commanded the whole environs and Fort George crowned the whole complex. An earthenware rampart — broad embankment — raised as a fortification on its seaside had four smaller half-ports — demi-bastions, surrounded by a dry moat, two palisades — or fences of pointed stakes for defense, a level protected area used for troops to patrol or assemble, and a gentle slope which ran downward from the fortification. There were four two-story blockhouses built into the stockade which surrounded the fortification.

Fort George defended the town, Pensacola. To defend Fort George itself, there stood on its upper height, looking over the low land to the west the Queen's Redoubt, a circular battery flanked on the north and south by recurving parapets. This advanced redoubt, just north of the stockade was 150 feet by 75 feet, with cannon mounted and a wet ditch. Three hundred yards below the Queen's Redoubt and 600 yards from Fort George stood an almost circular redoubt, the Prince of Wales Redoubt. A third redoubt, the Royal Navy Redoubt (also known as Barrancas Coloradas Fort), was located at a strategic distance from Fort George. This redoubt commanded the entrance to the bay, contained two batteries, one facing seaward and one aimed toward the entrance to the bay, and a powder magazine — a well-protected room in which gunpowder and other explosives were kept. Initially, it was garrisoned by German Waldeck mercenaries, and was built on the highest ground or summit of the Red Cliffs, over all the adjoining ground, with eleven pieces of cannon mounted thereon; five thirty-two pounders pointing towards the sea, two bearing towards the flanks, and the rest six pounders. The Queen's Redoubt, on the highest ground northwest of the Fort, housed fifty men and four cannon. It was considered the advanced redoubt and was surrounded by a ditch 26 feet wide and eight feet deep. The Prince of Wales Redoubt — or Middle Redoubt — was 300 yards north of the Fort and held between eight and ten cannon.

Major General John Campbell was the English commander of Fort George. He had a force of slightly less than 2,000 men; among them 300 German mercenaries, 272 American Loyalists, and possibly 300 Blacks. But roundabout the Fort, in the woodlands adjacent to it, especially on the north side, were to be found several hundred Indian warriors from the Appalachees, Creeks, Choctaws, Chikasaws, and Seminoles. These Indian allies of the British continually harassed and kept the Spanish forces on alert; their mission was to divert attention and firepower from Fort George. And, although the defenders of Fort George were considerably less in numbers than the attacking Spanish and French forces, Fort George was heavily fortified; it was well defended, as can be seen from the description of it above.

The Galveztown, Don Bernardo's armed brigantine, by Ethan Houser, 1991.

CHAPTER X

The Siege

On March 9, 1781, before dawn and under the cover of darkness, General de Gálvez landed his troops, Spanish Grenadiers and light infantry, ordnance and military stores on Santa Rosa Island, which he took without opposition. From there they proceeded to Sigüenza Point, site of an English redoubt which covered the entrance to the channel between the island and the mainland. This also was easily done and in the process seven English soldiers were taken prisoners. By March 11 a Spanish battery facing the Barrancas Coloradas Fort had been emplaced and a few days later another battery of two cannon was placed facing the English. By March 24, General de Gálvez and his troops moved form Bayou Grande to the east bank of Bayou Chico. It was at Bayou Chico that the Spanish forces made their first stand and built a series of small redoubts. Finally, the Spanish forces got themselves within 500 meters from enemy fortifications on one side and 800 meters on the other.

Early in March, almost two months prior to the definitive assault on Pensacola, General de Gálvez ordered Colonel Don José de Ezpeleta from Mobile and Lt. Colonel Pedro Piernas from New Orleans to converge on Pensacola with all men available in their respective commands. General de Gálvez, changing his mind, had now decided that the attack on Pensacola would be a dual land and sea attack. By March 23rd, reinforcements of 2,500 men had arrived in Pensacola under the command of the officers above. Two days later, the troops moved from Santa Rosa Island to the mainland.

While all this was taking place on the shores of Pensacola, General de Gálvez received the good news that his father, Don Matías, had also achieved significant successes in Central America, dislodging the English from the forts they held on the coasts of Honduras and Nicaragua.

Prior to the arrival of the reinforcements from New Orleans and Mobile, General de Gálvez on March 18 decided to force the entrance of the Spanish fleet into Pensacola Bay. He had decided it was time for his troops to set foot on the mainland. In the process, however, one of his ships was grounded on a sand bar. This and the previous similar problem he had also faced when leading the landing and attack on Mobile Bay caused the naval commander, Captain Don José de Calvo, to have doubts about his expertise in entering an enemy harbor. Don José de Calvo attempted to enter the bay himself but ran aground. Fearing for the safety of his fleet, Captain de Calvo refused to allow the ships to cross the shallow bar under the guns of the Red Cliffs Fort. Captain de Calvo, therefore, acting independently and under his own authority, refused to follow General de Gálvez's orders to enter the bay. To shame him into submission, General de Gálvez took matters into his own hands. Leading his own brig, the *Galveztown,* and the three other Louisiana vessels under his direct command, the two armed launches and the sloop, he crossed the bar and entered the channel. The English artillery at Fort Barrancas Coloradas opened fire upon the small fleet, but General de Gálvez and his small fleet of four vessels made it safely into the bay where they anchored under the shelter of the Spanish battery at Sigüenza Point.

Everywhere in the Spanish camp pandemonium broke loose. There was loud and enthusiastic cheering and a lot of *vivas* for General de Gálvez and his men. There had been a fifteen gun salute in their honor as they initiated their brave action. Now, there was a second fifteen gun salute to celebrate this great feat of General de Gálvez.

The next day, March 19, the rest of the Spanish squadron entered the bay. This heroic action was to merit for General de Gálvez, by royal decree, the addition of a pennant to his esutcheon, with the logo "Yo Solo," "I alone," (by myself) in commemoration of this heroic feat.

Don Bernardo de Gálvez leading his men to battle, by José Cisneros.

38

CHAPTER XI

Preparing for Battle

Basing his decision on a previous reconnaissance of the Pensacola Bay area by Captain Jacinto Panis, and on more recent intelligence he had been able to gather on the system of fortifications and defenses and the location of the harbor, powder magazines and warehouses, General de Gálvez laid out his tactical plan for the attack. General de Gálvez resolved to attack Pensacola by sea and not by land.

To accomplish this, however, General de Gálvez needed a well-equipped fleet from Havana. One obstacle to this was that the Navy commanders in Cuba were in disagreement with his strategy. The naval chief, Admiral Don Miguel de Goicoechea, recommended instead an advance on land towards the Río Perdido as "the best means to conquer the lace." The Río Perdido flows into the Gulf a few miles west of Pensacola. The Council in Havana was in agreement with the Naval Commander's recommendation. As a result, there soon developed a series of differences, delays and obstacles to General de Gálvez's plan.

Meanwhile, while General de Gálvez was beset with all these problems and obstacles placed in his path by the naval authorities in Cuba, the happenings in Spain were much different; the picture much brighter. In Spain there was intense and feverish excitement. They had heard the news of the victories on the Mississippi and General Bernardo de Gálvez's name was on everybody's lips. Spain was on a war-footing; all its energies directed and dedicated to the

task at hand in America. Innumerable officers and volunteers enlisted for service under General de Gálvez. Cities in Spain vied with
each other in collecting funds, clothing, medicines, and arms to
equip the ships for America. And, not only Spain contributed, the
inhabitants of Spanish America also contributed; even those in the
far-away California missions, at the initiative of Fray Junípero
Serra, contributed: "two pesos for each Spaniard and one for each
Indian." In Cuba, in 1780, through the efforts of Don Francisco de
Miranda, who was three decades later to become one of the libera-
tors of South America, "the amount of 1,200,000 pounds was col-
lected," to pay the French troops under General Rochambeau.
There also was a solidarity and financial support for the undertak-
ing in Florida from the Spanish Viceroyalties in Mexico, Lima,
Buenos Aires, and even from Manila in the far Pacific.

After much dissension and heated arguments and notwithstanding all the obstacles thrown on his path, General de Gálvez
was finally able to persuade Cuba's governor, Don Diego Navarro,
and Commanding General Navia and the War Council "to author-
ize 3,800 men to sail under his command with provisions for six
months, in addition to another 2,000 soldiers from Mexico." Re-
supply ships for Pensacola were to leave from Havana every two
weeks.

On October 16, 1780, with bells ringing and public prayers in
all churches, General de Gálvez and his fleet of troop ships departed from Havana, destination Pensacola. But, unbeknown and
unexpected by them, a terrible catastrophe awaited them. Two
days after leaving Havana, on October 18, one of those fierce,
howling, and destructive tropical storms, a hurricane, struck at
them. For the next six days, until it subsided on October 23, the
hurricane caused heavy losses to the expeditionary force, sank several ships, and scattered the rest throughout the Gulf Coast, some
as far as Yucatán in southeast Mexico. General de Gálvez and what
was left of his fleet were forced to return to Havana.

Undaunted by this tragic setback, General de Gálvez, with the
courage and sense of mission that was his characteristic, set about
reorganizing his second military expedition against Pensacola.
And, for the next four months he prepared. Again, he was faced
with tremendous obstacles. But, finally, he was ready for his second try. On February 28, 1781, General de Gálvez with a small
force of 1,315 men on board twenty troop ships departed from Ha-

vana. Escorting his troop ships were the man-of-war *San Ramón* — the flagship, three frigates and a packet-boat. The flagship was commanded by Admiral Don José de Calvo de Irazábal, with whom he was going to have serious difficulties later, especially before the landing of his forces in Pensacola.

Nine days later, after an uneventful voyage on the now calm waters of the Gulf of Mexico, General de Gálvez sighted the shores of Pensacola.

The hour had arrived for the great page of his life. Everything that had transpired up to now, the long months of arguments and disagreements, of inaction and delay, of perhaps secret jealousies, envies and dislikes, was behind. He was now ready for the great risk, perhaps the greatest triumph of his life.

GOLFO DE' MEXICO

1781 Map of Spanish Fleet entering Pensacola Bay.

CHAPTER XII

The Battle

Ever anxious to save lives, and considering that a frontal assault on Fort George would be too costly in lives, General de Gálvez, after intensive scouting and planning, prepared for a heavy bombardment of Fort George, by land and sea. Beginning on April 26, hundreds of his men were detailed to dig a covered trench from the Spanish lines to a small hill that commanded the heights above the Queen's Redoubt — also known as The Crescent because of its shape, and from there extend it to other redoubts that defended Fort George. As tunnels and trenches were dug and an encirclement of Fort George was thus effected, General de Gálvez had batteries placed in unforeseen positions to threaten vulnerable points. This seems to have been one of his favorite tactics. While some of this work was done at night, for obvious reasons, the English repeatedly shelled his positions by cannon and mortar fire. There were the inevitable casualties, the killed and the wounded. Eighteen of his men were killed like this on one occasion and others wounded; and this was not the only time.

On April 19, a formation of more than twenty Spanish ships was sighted very close to Pensacola. The naval commander of this fleet was Don José Solano, and under Field Marshal Don Juan Manuel Cagigal were another 1,600 reinforcements from Spain. Among these last reinforcements was the Hibernia Regiment, composed of 580 Irish Spanish soldiers. Accompanying the Spanish forces was a contingent of 725 French soldiers in four French frig-

43

ates. General de Gálvez now had a real army, an army of 5,940 men.

By early May 1781, Pensacola was completely surrounded, on land and by sea, by the combined Spanish and French forces. General de Gálvez was now ready for the final battle for Fort George. Spanish bombardment of Fort George began on May 6th and was answered in kind by the British. Assaults on some of the outer defenses and redoubts were to follow on the next day, but for some unforeseen circumstance they were not carried through. On the morning of May 8th, artillery fire opened up again. As fate would have it, one lucky shot from one of the Spanish batteries hit the powder magazine in the "Queen's Redoubt." A great explosion followed killing 105 British soldiers and wounding many more. This changed the whole situation dramatically. With the Queens Redoubt lost to the Spanish, General John Campbell realized he could no longer defend Fort George successfully as the Spanish forces were now in command of the heights above. At 2:30 P.M., four and a half hours after the fall of the Queen's Redoubt, General Campbell, in order to avoid further bloodshed of the military and civilians under his command, wrote to General de Gálvez and asked for cessation of hostilities until the next day, May 9th, at noon, at which time "articles of capitulation shall be considered and prepared." At 3:00 General Campbell had the white flag of surrender raised above Fort George.

The siege of Pensacola was over. Negotiations continued far into the night. At 1:00 A.M. on May 9, the generals came to an agreement. Under the terms of the Articles of Capitulation, "the British surrendered the entire province of British West Florida to Spain." In return, "the British troops and sailors would be allowed to go out with all the honors of war, arms shouldered, drums beating, flags flying." The victory of General de Gálvez in British West Florida was now complete.

On May 10th, at 3:00 P.M., the British marched out of the fort with full honors, as stipulated in the terms of surrender. Five hundred yards from the fort they stacked their arms in the customary ceremony prescribed for such occasions. Following this, the Spanish troops took possession of the fort. General de Gálvez had, once again, triumphed over the British.

Five months later — on October 19, 1781, British General Lord Charles Cornwallis, after his defeat at the famous and historic battle, the final battle of the American Revolution, at Yorktown in

Granadero de Gálvez in full uniform, 1770s–1780s, by John Houser, 1991.

Virginia, surrendered his entire force of 7,000 men to American General George Washington and his army of "5,700 Continental soldiers, 3,100 Virginia militia, and 7,000 French troops." The American Revolution, also known as the American War of Independence, was over.

Some historians have claimed that General Bernardo de Gálvez, by his victory at Pensacola, had speeded the final outcome of the American Revolution, for through his victory over the British at Pensacola he had helped to bring this about.

General de Gálvez had indeed established a second front in the South that helped to alleviate the pressure that General George Washington and his other generals were feeling in the battlefields along the east coast, in the Ohio Valley, and around the Great Lakes region, as well as in the Southern colonies, especially the Carolinas and Georgia. The actions of General de Gálvez in the Floridas, in Louisiana and in the middle and lower Mississippi had tangible and positive results, results highly beneficial to the American patriots.

As we close this chapter let us remember that the Spanish triumphs at Manchak, Baton Rouge, Natchez, Mobile, and Pensacola, contributed greatly to the final victory of the Americans over the British and the final consummation of the independence of the infant nation, the new republic, the United States of America.

As a reward for his victory at Pensacola more and greater honors were bestowed on General Bernardo de Gálvez by King Carlos III. By royal decree, General de Gálvez was now given the titles of Count de Gálvez and Viscount of Galveztown, in addition to his own special and distinctive coat of arms. General de Gálvez was further promoted to the rank of Lieutenant General and was also commissioned as Governor of West Florida, while at the same time he was to continue being Governor of Louisiana.

Everywhere in Europe and in the Americas people heard of his great feats in the Gulf Coast. General Bernardo de Gálvez was the hero of the day throughout the Spanish-speaking world, and, then, too, in the new nation, the United States of America.

CHAPTER XIII

His Last Campaign

Following the expulsion of the British from the Gulf Coast General de Gálvez proceeded to wage war against the English in the Bahamas. British privateers had long used the Bahamas as a base of operations, to prey against the Spanish towns along the Gulf Coast, in the Caribbean, in Central America and in the ports of northern South America. By January of 1782, General de Gálvez had cleared all this vast area from British intrusions.

His next orders from Madrid were for him to move with an army of 10,000 men and set upon the conquest of Jamaica, the last British bastion in the Caribbean Sea. As ordered, he moved with his troops to Guarico, in the island of Santo Domingo, and prepared for the expedition against Jamaica. He was poised and ready, but while awaiting for the arrival of the French fleet, as this was to be a joint Spanish and French action, the warring nations, France, Spain, and the United States, arrived at peace terms with the British and signed the Treaty of Paris of 1783. This put an end to the conflict between England on one side and Spain, France, and the new United States of America on the other. King George III of England officially recognized the independence of the new nation, the United States of America, and further agreed to cede the two Floridas, East and West, to Spain. And, it was while stationed in Santo Domingo that the only male child of the de Gálvezes, Miguel, was born to Marie Felicité and Bernardo.

This was the end of one of the most important chapters in his

47

life, and now . . . Following the peace accords, in April 1783 General de Gálvez, accompanied by his family and by some of his troops, embarked for Spain after eight years of uninterrupted service in America. He was to enjoy but a brief respite, a few months rest in his homeland. In October 1784, the Crown once again called him and entrusted him with another big responsibility. The King named him Governor and Captain-General of Cuba, and Royal Inspector General of Troops — regular and militias — in the Indies. He soon departed from Madrid, accompanied by his wife and children, to assume his new duties in Havana, the capital of Cuba.

CHAPTER XIV

In Cuba, and then
...Mexico

He was to serve in his new position for only three short months. King Carlos III appointed him to replace his recently deceased father as Viceroy in Mexico City.

General Bernardo de Gálvez was by now known throughout the Spanish-speaking world; everywhere popular, the hero of the day. Mexico received him in triumph. The Mexicans already knew him and liked him, for he had served in Mexico between the years of 1765 to 1771. They knew the illustrious de Gálvez family, for his father, Matías, had also been a well-liked Viceroy. Furthermore, the Visitador de las Indias, his Uncle José, was also well-known and highly respected in Mexico. The Mexicans now expected even greater things of the son and the nephew of his great predecessors.

Upon his arrival in Mexico, at the Gulf port city off Veracruz on May 21, 1785, he was acclaimed by the populace, high and low. Next, his official entrance to Mexico City was a truly royal and gigantic parade, a veritable triumph, a victory march. Solemn yet joyous, the military in their resplendent uniforms and the dignitaries of the Church in their ceremonial attire, flowered triumphal arches everywhere, flags and banners flying in the breeze, military bands and the native musicians in their regional dress, Te Deums in the Cathedral and church bells ringing everywhere, fireworks, delegations from all segments of the population, *vivas* and more *vivas*, a gigantic victory procession. General Bernardo de Gálvez was now, in addition to all his other innumerable titles and honors, the Viceroy of New Spain, Spain's jewel in the Americas.

The Coat of Arms authorized for Don Bernardo and the House of Gálvez bestowed upon him for his exploits in the New World by King Carlos III. From Reales Cédulas (decrees), 1783. From the Historic New Orleans Collection.

CHAPTER XV

As Viceroy
of New Spain

The expectations of the Mexicans were well-founded and proven true in no time. A severe famine, caused by the loss of crops due to heavy frosts in the winter of 1785, struck the land early in 1786. The new Viceroy, General Bernardo de Gálvez, immediately became involved in trying to alleviate the suffering. He used his own funds to buy grain for the needy. He plunged into the work of distributing the grain and other types of aid to the needy himself, without paying any attention to protocol. Needless to say, this further endeared him to the masses of the destitute. Here, amongst them and in their midst was the Viceroy, providing whatever aid he could; rations of beans, rice, and corn; aid given with a smile and a happy heart. Here was a truly remarkable human being, a true humanitarian, a man that loved the subjects of his King. This was Bernardo de Gálvez. He even gave the homeless, who had moved to the capital in search of food, lodging in the patios of the Palace, maintaining them at his own expense. He truly was a man with a heart.

To remedy all the calamities that usually accompany a famine, General de Gálvez furnished seeds for replanting to the peasants, intensified a system of public works, opened highways, paved streets, completed the construction of the towers of the Cathedral and, among many other initiatives, distributed something almost unheard of at the time — the vaccine against smallpox, a disease usually fatal to the indigenous population.

51

The chronicles of the day also say: "He liked to look well and to be seen." "He was young and gallant." "He was frank and at ease with people." "His was a merry character, anxious for activity." "He enjoyed being with the people; strolling the streets, attending spectacles, especially bullfights." And, having in his stay in France developed a liking for French style coffee, "café au lait," "café con leche," (coffee with sugared milk), he introduced that practice to Mexico. The Mexicans loved it immediately and "café con leche" has remained popular in Mexico to this day.

He also liked and enjoyed the finer things, the arts in all their forms. He also sponsored higher caliber cultural activities: the opera, the theatre, poetry recitals, the ballet, lectures, concerts, and classical music. It was customary to see him accompanied to all these cultural activities by his elegant and charming wife, María Feliciana de Saint-Maxent de Gálvez, lovingly called "la Francesita" by the Mexicans, being as she was a New Orleans creole.

He enjoyed driving his carriage along the Alameda and the Paseo de Bucareli, the elegant boulevards of the day. Everywhere he went he was immediately recognized and acclaimed. He always responded warmly to the people. They loved him, and he loved them, too.

At the bullfights he enjoyed "throwing gold doubloons wrapped in silk handkerchiefs to the matadors." This had never been done before. It was a first, as it also was for him to drive himself and his wife and children around the bullring in a small carriage, waving to the people and acknowledging their enthusiasm. The people simply went wild, showing in their enthusiasm and their admiration the affection they felt for him and his family. He always insisted that in the bullfights the cuadrillas and the matadors be equally represented, insofar as possible, by both Spanish and Mexicans. This is one more proof of his sense of political adeptness. Another first of his day and time: in the November 1785 bullfighting season there were a total of twenty fights, morning and afternoon. A total of six women participated in some of these fights. To one of the woman bullfighters he gave 100 pesos for "her art and skill." And, after the fights, besides all sorts of entertainment, the bullfights would always be followed by a dance in the ring.

There were other examples illustrating his kind heart and generosity. On one occasion he helped some of his soldiers put out a fire in the barracks on the Palace grounds in the middle of the night. He rushed out of his palace, clad in his night shirt, ready to

The Metropolitan Cathedral of Mexico City and the Castillo de Chapultepec, Vicere-gal residence. The towers of the Cathedral and the Castillo were both completed through Don Bernardo's efforts.

help in the action. Another time he donated his carriage to a poor priest so that he would not have to go on foot to give the last ministrations of the Church to the sick and the dying. Also, being naturally religious and devout, he attended holy Mass daily in his private chapel. Not being ostentatious, though, he kept his attendance at the religious solemnities in the Cathedral to a minimum.

It should be noted, too, that through his efforts the reconstruction and completion of Chapultepec Castle was effected. He asked and obtained from Carlos III authorization to complete this project and, in so doing, was responsible for what we today know as the Castle of Chapultepec; what was to become seven decades later the official residence of Archduke Maximilian of Austria and Princess Carlota of Belgium, his wife, in their tragic and futile attempt to become the Emperor and Empress of Mexico. After Maximilian and Carlota, the Castle of Chapultepec became the official residence of the Presidents of Mexico up until the 1950s. Today, the Castle of Chapultepec in Mexico City is the pride and joy — and a showcase — of the Mexican nation. Begun in the 18th century as a viceregal residence, Chapultepec Castle has also served as an imperial palace and a presidential mansion. It now serves as a museum of Mexico's long history. Likewise, the imposing towers of the Metropolitan Cathedral of Mexico City were completed under the energetic leadership of the Viceroy.

Another episode in the life of Viceroy Bernardo de Gálvez revolves around a pardon he granted to several criminals who were about to be hanged as "thieves and murderers." As luck would have it, on the Saturday preceding Palm Sunday in the Spring of 1786, Bernardo happened to pass by the Plaza de Concha and noticed the gallows that had been erected. Upon inquiring as to the happenings he was told what was about to take place. Out of a sense of pity and compassion, he granted pardons, which were later upheld by the Crown, to the convicts. And, on another occasion he ordered a haughty parish priest to give religious burial to a poor Indian whose wife could not afford to pay for the church service. He even volunteered to sing the responses at the service as the priest claimed he could not conduct the service because he did not have the singers needed for the ceremony. Viceroy Bernardo served as the cantor at the service. These and many more are examples of his humanity, his true greatness, and of his compassion for those in need. He was truly a great and sincere man, a true gentleman; a man with a big heart.

CHAPTER XVI

Bernardo's
Instrucción de 1786

In his *Instrucción de 1786,* Bernardo, now Viceroy of New Spain, was to set the policy which was to guide and become Spain's official Indian policy in the northern territories throughout the remainder of the Spanish period (to 1821). Said document, the *Instruction of 1786,* was dated August 26, 1786; merely three months before his untimely death in Mexico City.

Bernardo, who had first served as a lieutenant with his uncle José's expeditionary force in Sonora from 1768 to 1770, and a short time later as a *compañía volante* captain in Chihuahua and as military commander for both Nueva Vizcaya (now the Mexican state of Chihuahua and Southwest Texas) and Sonora from 1770 to 1771, formulated his policy, *Instructions for Governing the Interior Provinces of New Spain,* after much careful and serious thought and consideration. Having, in six long years of direct contact, learned the ways of the Indians of the northern territories, Bernardo now — through this document — made the recommendations that became Spain's guidelines in dealing with the Indians of the northern territories.

Bernardo, although deeply sensitive and humanitarian as a person, had found no other way of dealing effectively with the aborigines of the northern territories. As a practical military man, Bernardo was now convinced that this was the wise and right policy for him and his successors to follow in working and/or dealing with the Indians. Bernardo urged a policy alternating a vigorous military prosecution with peaceful persuasion and economic assistance. In

55

the process of pacification, Bernardo urged that diplomatic and economic enticement, coupled with military escalation, be used concurrently; peace pacts and alliances were to be effected with those Indian tribes and/or nations so willing. Tribes who kept their treaties with the Spaniards were to be given preferential treatment. The objective, however, was to make them dependent on the Spanish. To those tribes who did not accept the Spanish Peace, discord and division as already existed among them was to be exploited to the fullest, so as to further weaken them. And, to those tribes who rejected the "Spanish Peace," incessant war against them became the order of the day. Viceroy Bernardo de Gálvez also regularized a procedure long in practice, "bestowing gifts upon Indians who came in to make peace." All these actions towards the Indians would be conducted directly by the military commanders themselves, in order to prevent any serious misunderstandings which might endanger the peace. Ultimately, this in itself would make possible a reduction in the number of troops. Thus, lowering the cost of military operations would, in itself, be enough to subsidize the peace itself.

In regards to the Spanish troops themselves, the commanders of the three northern territories were authorized to deal with emergencies first and reporting afterwards, thereby increasing their internal efficiency. Greater autonomy was also given to the regional commanders to deal with any and all military matters within their jurisdiction. Also, the commanders were urged to greater efforts at inspiring both officers and men with a deep devotion to the service and to greater achievements; with the incentive and certainty that their efforts would be both recognized and rewarded, regardless of their social category. These, then, became the bases of the policy that was to be followed in the military service of Spain in the northern territories.

Bernardo also established a militia tax in the more established communities so as to alleviate the cost of military operations on the Crown. This would also tend to make the local communities who could well afford it, more responsive and responsible for the defense of their perimeters.

To increase the effectiveness of the forces in the presidios, Bernardo now held the company captains and officers personally responsible for the least carelessness on their part. Repeated negligence would cost them their commands or ranks. Furthermore, any damage sustained by the presidios would have to be paid for or replaced at their own expense. Regularity of reconnaissance was established, schedules of patrol forces were varied so as to catch the enemy off guard or by surprise, and the pursuit of marauding Indians was to be prompt and swift. All presidio troops possible would be activated, and lower-paid Indian "auxiliares" would also be utilized. A new and more realistic pay-scale for the officers and troops was also enacted, so as to make their hard career more palatable and attractive to his men. Thus, his men would also be happier and more content, and thereby more efficient in the performance of their duties.

Bernardo's directives were soon proven so wise and effective that they were implemented. His instructions that manageable detachments of from 150 to 200 troops were to be used in the Indian campaigns proved invaluable; as well as his directive that only officers of proven merit, valor, experience, and knowledge of the terrain, regardless of rank or seniority, were to be placed in command of military detachments.

Bernardo's *Instrucción de 1786* became binding as a royal ordinance with the King's approval on March 20, 1787, by the "Real Orden de El Pardo."

CHAPTER XVII

His Death
in Mexico City

Bernardo's fruitful and generous life came to a premature end.
His untimely death cut short his potential to become one of Mexico's most outstanding viceroys. In October of 1786 he became mortally sick of an illness that in a few weeks was to end his life. An epidemic, probably of scarlet fever or diphtheria, struck Mexico City.
It spread like wildfire. By mid-October, the *viaticum* was administered to him by the Dean of the Cathedral, in the presence of the
Archbishop of Mexico. His spiritual advisor, priest and confessor,
had already prepared him for his death journey, according to the
rites of the Catholic Church, of which he was a most loyal and devoted son. And, against the advice of his physicians, Bernardo
arose from his sick bed, had himself dressed in the full uniform of a
Lieutenant General and Field Marshal, with all the regalia, sashes
and insignia symbolic of his office and all his military decorations,
and received the Sacrament. He was ready, ready to go. He lingered between life-and-death for another six weeks. But, finally, on
November 30, 1786, at daybreak, he died. He was forty years old,
in the prime of life and the bloom of youth. He died in the Palace of
the Archbishop in Tacubaya, at that time one of Mexico City's suburbs. To make medical and spiritual help more readily available to
him in his illness, he had been moved there from Chapultepec. The
Archbishop's Palace was completely surrounded by the saddened
multitudes who had gathered, notwithstanding the rain, to pray for
their Viceroy. Through their tears many a prayer was said, first for

59

his recovery, and when death came, for the repose of his soul. The people were simply returning the love that he had given to them, for he truly had been their friend, their benefactor, their Viceroy. He was one of the best Viceroys Mexico had ever known.

Mexico City, the capital of New Spain, was in deep mourning. Hundreds of church bells tolled, carrying the sad news to all the distant corners of the Valley of Anáhuac. Fast couriers were dispatched swiftly to all the provincial capitals of New Spain to convey the sad news of the Viceroy's passage.

He made his last entrance into the capital, Mexico City, amid the tolling of church bells, the thunder of cannon, and the plaintive dirges asking God's mercy on his soul. His body, in full uniform, was placed in a carriage, accompanied by equerries bearing torches. His truly saddened troops rendered their last salutes, with great pride but with a heavy heart. Military honors were the order of the day. The Archbishop and all his clergy received his body at the foot of the steps to the entrance of Mexico's Metropolitan Cathedral. The church rituals were most appropriate for the sad occasion.

In his Last Will and Testament General Bernardo de Gálvez had asked that he be buried alongside his father, in the Franciscan Church of San Fernando. This was done; his wish was honored. However, at the request of his wife, his heart was placed in a gold urn and placed beneath the altar of the Santos Reyes in the Cathedral of Mexico City.

CHAPTER XVIII

His Family

Two months after his death, his wife, María Feliciana de Saint-Maxent *Vda.* (viuda-widow) de Gálvez, gave birth to their third child, a girl, in Mexico City. She was named Guadalupe in honor of the Patroness of Mexico, Our Lady of Guadalupe. The Mexicans were elated. They celebrated the birth of the child of their recently dead beloved Viceroy Bernardo de Gálvez. Rich and expensive gifts were given in memory of and in gratitude to Bernardo de Gálvez on behalf of "the most noble City of Mexico" by the Cabildo, the City Council, to the baby Guadalupe, to the widow, and to the other children. After their great sadness at Bernardo's death, there was now great rejoicing at his daughter's birth. As little Guadalupe de Gálvez de Saint-Maxent was being christened the Cathedral bells pealed joyously. Everybody understood the reason and the message.

The torch of the de Gálvez family was not to burn too long after that, however. Fate decreed, as the poet Manrique says, "that the torch be extinguished when the fire burned most brightly." Bernardo's father, Matías, had died in 1784. Two of Bernardo's uncles, Miguel and Antonio, had died previously. His famous mentor, his Uncle José, was to survive Bernardo by just one year. The Marquis of Sonora, Don José de Gálvez, died in 1787. None of his uncles left any direct male descendants, and Bernardo's only son, Miguel, who inherited his title, died "a youth and single."

Little is known about his daughters Matilde and Guadalupe. One source says that Matilde emigrated to Italy.

The illustrious de Gálvez family just faded away. As an anonymous Spanish poet, who evidently much loved and admired Bernardo and the de Gálvez dynasty, has said, "They went down as they came up, like a sigh. The de Gálvez just melted away."

BERNARDO DE GÁLVEZ
1746-1786

Another drawing of Don Bernardo de Gálvez by Abel Ramírez, 1991.

CHAPTER XIX

Recognition at Last
for Bernardo de Gálvez

As we already know, General Bernardo de Gálvez received many well-deserved honors and awards from his King in recognition of his victories in the Mississippi and on the Gulf Coast. Bernardo became a legend even in his own lifetime.

American statesmen of that epoch also realized — and acknowledged — that through his invaluable and generous assistance the victory of the American rebels was made possible much sooner. Benjamin Franklin, Thomas Jefferson, and Patrick Henry, all leaders of the Colonial Revolt, so said in their correspondence with General de Gálvez. From General Charles Lee of Virginia there also is acknowledgment of that fact. In a letter from General George Washington to His Catholic Majesty Carlos III of Spain, there is additional testimony of all this.

It is time that all Americans become aware of Bernardo de Gálvez's and Spain's contributions to the American Revolution. This is the reason for this short monograph.

Fortunately, since the American Bicentennial in 1976, we have been hearing more about this almost forgotten chapter in our nation's history. This is the time to remember.

In a commemorative booklet issued in 1983, "Hispanics in America's Defense: an Overview, Secretary of Defense Caspar W. Weinberger, recognizes Bernardo de Gálvez and says: "Americans have not forgotten Bernardo de Gálvez. Though a loyal citizen of Spain, he contributed greatly to the founding of our New Nation."

The Texas Legislature also officially acknowledged Bernardo de Gálvez and Spain in House Concurrent Resolution No. 30, adopted by the House on June 29, 1984, and by the Senate on June 30, and signed by Governor Mark White on July 3, 1984. Yes, Americans are beginning to remember this important period in our nation's history.

In the 1990 legislative session of the Florida State Legislature, both the House and the Senate of that state passed a concurrent resolution drafted by Dr. Frank de Varona, Associate Superintendent of Dade County Public Schools in Miami, recognizing General de Gálvez and the role of Hispanics in the American Revolution. Said resolution urged the sixty-seven school districts in Florida to include this important chapter in our nation's history in the present courses of study in kindergarten through the twelfth grade. Consul General Erik L. Martel worked closely with Dr. de Varona in this important project.

An equestrian statue of Bernardo de Gálvez is in our nation's capital, Washington, D.C.; another stands in the Spanish Plaza in New Orleans, and a third one is in the Spanish Plaza in Mobile, Alabama. A portrait of the hero hangs in the Capitol of Louisiana in Baton Rouge, and a bust is in the Gálvez Park. A historical plaque commemorates the peaceful surrender of Fort Panmure's garrison of eighty men at Natchez, as agreed to by Colonel Dickson in signing the articles of capitulation following the Battle of Baton Rouge. The October 5, 1779, marker is a highly visible memorial located in the historical district of the city of Natchez, Mississippi. A second Gálvez bust was dedicated by the City of Pensacola, Florida, during Bicentennial Ceremonies on May 10, 1981, in a small park with a sectional reconstruction of Fort George at its original site.

In July 1980, the U.S. Postal Service issued a commemorative stamp in the American Revolution Heroes Series to honor General Bernardo de Gálvez on the bicentennial of Spain's Victory at the Battle of Mobile. And, on November 30, 1986, in observance of the 200th anniversary of his death in Mexico City, the Granaderos unveiled and dedicated two plaques to General de Gálvez; one in the Old Archbishop's Palace in Tacubaya, where he died, and the other at the Iglesia de San Fernando where he is buried.

In the city of Pensacola, Florida, scene of the most brilliant successes of General de Gálvez, the Spanish Museum holds a large number of mementos of him and Spanish colonial Florida.

WAGED SUCCESSFUL CAMPAIGNS
AGAINST THE BRITISH DURING
THE AMERICAN REVOLUTION

GENERAL
BERNARDO DE GÁLVEZ
1746-1786
GOVERNOR OF SPANISH LOUISIANA

Bernardo leading his men on the Siege of Pensacola.

CHAPTER XX

Concluding Comments

In summation, it can be said that Bernardo de Gálvez embodied and exemplified the mission and driving force of the noblest and truest Spanish tradition of his time, which is best summarized by the motto: "Por Dios y por el Rey" (for God and King). All his endeavors were guided by this noble and exalted principle.

Having chosen the military career as his life vocation at the early age of sixteen, Bernardo's whole life was going to revolve around his commitment to his country and his King. He served his King on three contents: Europe, the Americas, and Africa. In all three he shed his blood for the cause he believed in and to which he was committed. Furthermore, he drove the British from the Gulf of Mexico and helped in the birth of a new nation, the United States of America, soon to become the most powerful nation on earth. Through his invaluable assistance he helped to make this possible.

I would like to close this true story by reflecting on a question that is often asked by those who have been fortunate to hear about General Bernardo de Gálvez and his military feats on the Gulf Coast and the Mississippi, and his great victory at the Battle of Pensacola. The question asked usually goes like this: "Why is the Battle of Pensacola significant in our study of the American Revolution? What makes it so special, so different?"

The answer lies in the fact that it weakened Britain's hold on its southern colonies and, in so doing, helped to alleviate the pressure that General George Washington and his generals were feeling in the east. It cut off the British access to the important and navigable Mississippi River. It sealed off the British in the southern colonies. That was its primary importance.

Secondly, Pensacola was the scene of a brilliantly executed campaign which some historians interpret as the turning point of the war. In the final year of the American Revolution, battles were fought in the Southern Front, along the lower Mississippi and on the Gulf Coast, by soldiers and seamen of various nationalities — none of whom wore the uniform of the American Continental Army. None of the Thirteen Colonies in rebellion against King George III of England was involved in these particular battles. Pensacola was hundreds of miles south of the battlefields of the American Revolution.

The Anglo-Spanish conflict on the Gulf Coast diminished British influence in the strategic borderlands and the lower Mississippi Valley. Also, it kept desperately needed British regiments from the last campaigns which resulted in the American victory at Yorktown.

That, in brief, is the basic importance of the Battle of Pensacola; why it was special and how it was different. And, in addition to the historic significance of the Battle of Pensacola, it should be remembered that the American colonists were greatly aided by Spain in their quest for freedom. This aid to the 13 American Colonies came from Spain in several forms: monetary grants, credits, outright gifts of uniforms, arms and ammunition, cannons and cannonballs, lead and gunpowder, food, medical supplies, tents and blankets; whatever was needed and requested by the American military commanders.

Spain's contributions towards the independence of the United States of America is a fact which is finally being recognized as an integral part in our American heritage and one more glorious chapter in our nation's fight for freedom.

The American nation has realized that it indeed owes much to General Bernardo de Gálvez, and that General Bernardo de Gálvez truly is one of our nation's great heroes.

Likewise, it is proper that we remember in a special way during the Quintcentenary of the Encounter of Two Peoples Spain's gigantic efforts in the New World, the Americas. Spain led in all areas: the discovery, exploration, settlement, Christianization, and in the integration — whether by assimilation or acculturation — of the American natives to European culture.

As a result or consequence of the above, Hispanics have played an active part in the development of this great country. The Spanish and their descendants were in many parts of what is now the United States one hundred years before the Pilgrims landed at Plymouth Rock. The Spanish and their descendants in the New World led in the exploration and settlement of the Americas: North, Central, and South. The Hispanic peoples are an integral part of these United States; they have helped in its development. They are Americans in every sense of the word, truly and true Americans.

Glossary

Definitions are appropriate to the time frame of the story.

aborigines — the native Americans; the Indians

accede — to be in agreement, in accord

adhesion — the act of agreeing to unite; sticking together

aligned — on the side of; allied

alleviate — to lighten the load or impact; to make more bearable

ancestors — the ones who came before

animosity — strong dislike

archives — official government records

audacity — daring; boldness

bastion — bulwark; a projecting defense in a fortification

batteries — cannon emplacements on a rampart

Berbers — light-skinned descendants of ancient Semitic peoples of the Mediterranean coast of North Africa

blockhouse — sentry post

booty — spoils (gains) of war taken from the enemy

bullion — gold or silver cast in bars or ingots for later reshaping or remelting

cabildo — Spanish for City Council

calamities — a series of unfortunate events

cantor — one who leads — or chants — prayers in a church service

capitulation — surrender

Captain-General — a title of very high rank in the Spanish Army

chronicles — written accounts

collaboration — help given; cooperation

compañía volante — a small — fast and light — cavalry unit

concession — a special privilege, or franchise — granted by the government

concocted — plotted

confluence — the point where two rivers meet and start flowing together

consummation — the realization of a goal or objective; accomplishment

71

contraband — smuggled — illegal — goods

count — a nobleman of rank; title of nobility

courier — messenger

Crown (the) — the King; the King's government

cuadrillas — in bullfighting, the bullfighter's entourage

detachments — small military units

destitute — extremely poor; in very great need

dirges — mournful funeral chants or music

discord — intense disagreements

diversionary — something that distracts or calls attention away from

doubloons — a former gold coin of Spain worth, at that time, about 100 centavos (cents)

environs — the surrounding area

equerries — mounted and uniformed attendants to royalty

exacerbates — to make harsher, more violent or severe

gallows — the place set up for the hanging of criminals

haughty — one who likes to impress others with his/her high social status;
snobbish

humanism — respect and liking for fellow humans, regardless of their social
status

illustrious — famous; well-known and respected for personal merits

immersed — totally involved in an activity

imminent — about to happen or take place

incessant — never-stopping

indigo — a blue dye obtained from several plants

intelligence — the gathering of military information

intrusions — forays into enemy territory

lineage — family line of noble (aristocratic) descent

marauding — pillaging; thieving

maritime — having to do — or related — to the sea

Mass — the main and most important Catholic worship service

matador — a full-fledged bullfighter

mentor — a trusted advisor; a valued counselor

mercenaries — soldiers serving a foreign government for pay

merchantmen — merchant ships

militia — a body of volunteers organized in military companies at local or state
level

moat — for defensive purposes, a trench — or canal — filled with water and
surrounding a fortification

neutrality — not taking sides, politically or ideologically

pacification — pacifying; establishing peace — law and order — in any given
area

palatable — agreeable; more acceptable

pandemonium — a loud — disorderly — commotion

peso — a former silver coin of Spain, equivalent to 100 centavos (cents)

plot — a secret plan

pound sterling — a paper monetary unit of the United Kingdom (Great Britain) equivalent to about $2.40 U.S. dollars

powder magazine — a room where gunpowder is stored

privateers — privately owned armed ships commissioned by a government to fight or harass enemy shipping

prizes of war — war booty; captured enemy ships and their cargo

province — a large geographical area or a political subdivision of a kingdom

quinine — medicine used in the treatment of malaria

rampart — a mound of earth used as a bulwark — or defense — around a fortification

real — a former Spanish silver coin equivalent to a dollar

reconnaisance — an inspection of a given area for military purposes

redoubt — a strategically placed defense position

refuge — a haven; a safe place

regalia — full vestments or uniform of any given office: church, royal, or military

reprisal — retaliation against an enemy

respite — an interval of relief; a brief rest

sacrament — an important and specific ritual — or practice — in the Catholic Church

shod — to supply footwear (shoes, boots, etc.)

stipulation — agreed upon terms in a treaty or contract

strategy — military plan

suppress — to do away with, by authority or by force

tactic — military maneuver or procedure

tangible — something that can be seen

Te-Deum — a solemn hymn of praise and thanksgiving to God for a special victory or favor

treaty — a formal agreement entered into by governments

Viceroy — the highest personal representative of the King in a colony

vied — competed with others

visitador — a royal inspector in the Spanish colonies

viva — a joyous and loud popular Spanish acclamation of approval especially for a high government official; "Long live . . .!"

vulnerable — weak; an area of weakness

Bibliography

Boeta, José Rodulfo. *Bernardo de Gálvez.* Madrid: Publicaciones Españolas, 1977.

Caughey, James Walton. *Bernardo de Gálvez in Louisiana, 1776–1783.* Berkeley: University of California Press, 1934.

Cottrell, John and the Editors of Time-Life Books. *The Great Cities/Mexico City.* Amsterdam: Time-Life International (Nederland) 1979.

Divine, Robert A., Breen, T. H. Frederickson, G. M., Williams, R. Hal. *America Past and Present.* Glenview, Illinois: Scott, Foresman & Co., 1987.

Faye, Stanley. "The Spanish and British Fortifications of Pensacola 1698–1821." Pensacola: Pensacola Historical Society Quarterly, Volume 6, Number 4, April 1972.

Fernández y Fernández, Enrique. *Spain's Contribution to the Independence of the United States.* Washington: Embassy of Spain, 1985.

Livermore, Henry. *A History of Spain.* New York: Minerva Press, 1968.

McWilliams, Carey. *North From Mexico.* New York: Praeger Publishers, 1990.

Martel, Erik Ignacio. *Apuntes Sobre la Fundación de la Orden de Granaderos de Gálvez.* Coral Gables, Florida: Consulado General de España, June 1991.

Moorhead, Max L. *The Presidio — Bastion of the Spanish Borderlands.* Norman: University of Oklahoma Press, 1975.

Parkes, Henry B. *A History of Mexico.* Boston: Houghton Mifflin Company, 1969.

Parks, Virginia. *Siege! Spain and Britain: Battle of Pensacola March 9–May 8, 1781.* Pensacola: Pensacola Historical Society, 1981.

Riva, Palacio, Gen. D. Vicente. *Mexico a Traves de los Siglos, Vol. II.* México, D.F.: Editorial Cumbre S.A., 7th edition, 1953.

Salvat, Juan. *Historia de Mexico,* Vols. 4 and 5. Mexico, D.F.: Salvat Editores de México, S.A., 1974.

Servies, James A., *The Siege of Pensacola, 1781. A Bibliography*. Pensacola: The Gálvez Commission of the City of Pensacola, 1981.

Sierra, Justo. *The Political Evolution of the Mexican People*. Translated by Charles Ramsdell. Austin: University of Texas Press, 1969.

Thonhoff, Robert H. *The Texas Connection with the American Revolution*. Austin: Eakin Press, 1981.

Tiner, Nancy Reynolds. *Bernardo de Gálvez* "Unsung Hero." Brochure published by the Texas Society, Daughters of the American Revolution and printed for distribution by the San Antonio, Texas, Chapter of the Damas de Gálvez, 1985.

United States Department of Defense. *Hispanics in America's Defense*. Washington: 1983.

Woodward, Jr., Ralph Lee. *Tribute to Don Bernardo de Gálvez*. Baton Rouge: Moran Industries, Incorporated, 1979.

Wright, J. Leitch, Jr. *Anglo-Spanish Rivalry in North America*. Athens: University of Georgia Press, 1971.

Yela Utrilla, Juan Francisco. *España Ante la Independencia de los Estados Unidos*. Madrid: Publicaciones Españolas, 1970.